teach me about

# The Dentist

Copyright © Joy Berry, 2022
Originally Published, 1986

All rights are reserved.

No part of this book can be duplicated or used without the prior written permission of the copyright owner, except for the use of brief quotations from the book.

For inquiries or permission requests contact the publisher.

Published by Joy Berry Enterprises
www.joyberryenterprises.com

teach me about

# The Dentist

### By JOY BERRY

*Illustrated by Bartholomew*

Some dentists are women.

Some dentists are men.

My dentist is a man.

I am going to visit my dentist to find out whether or not my teeth are OK.

I go to the dentist's office to see my dentist.

I have to wait in the waiting room until it is my turn to see him.

The dental assistant is a person who helps the dentist. She takes me to another room. There are many things in this room.

I sit in a special chair.

The dentist comes into the room.

He shines a big light on my teeth.

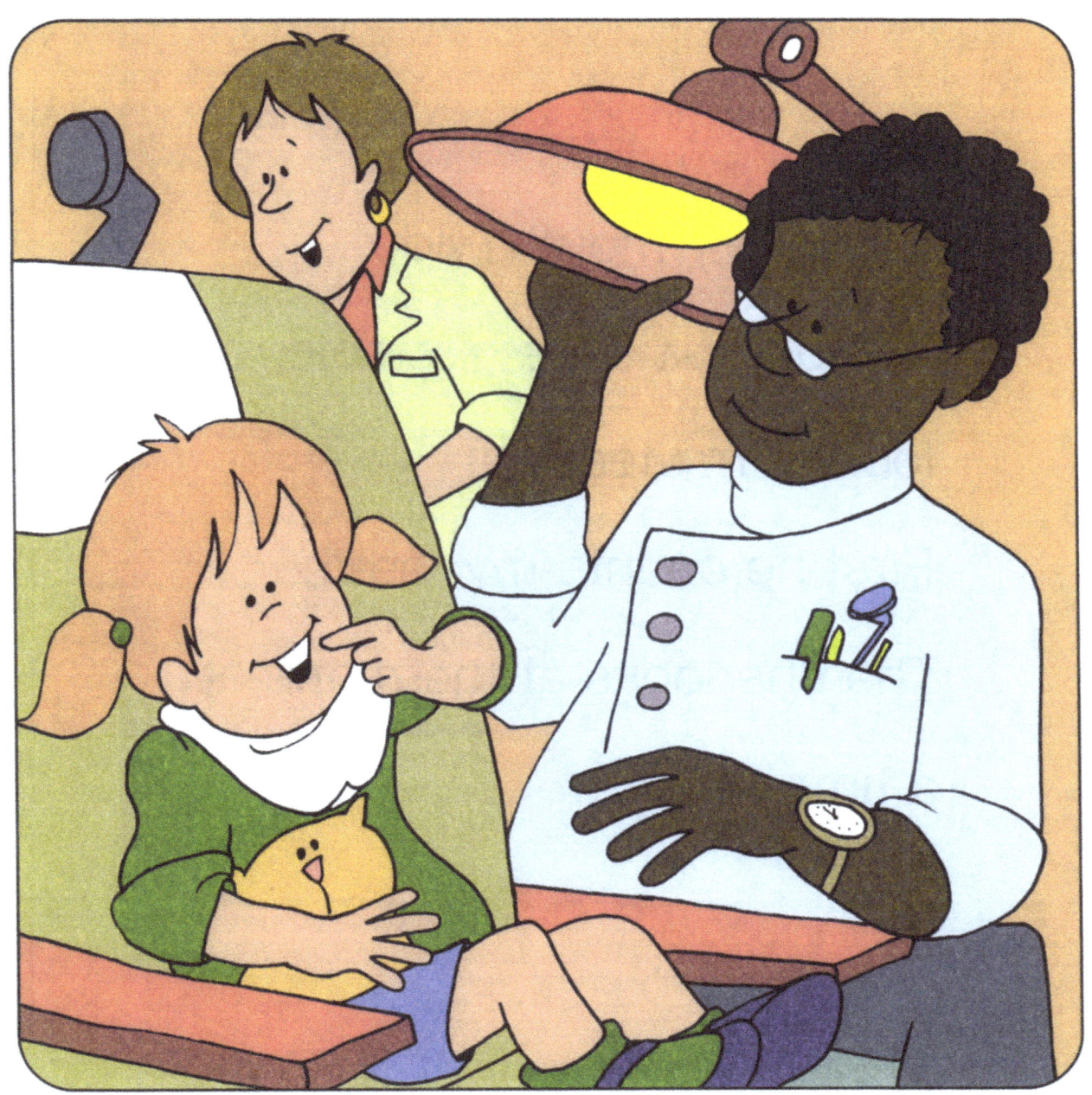

I open my mouth wide.

The dentist uses his tools to look at my teeth.

First he counts my teeth.

Then he looks at them one at a time.

The dentist tells me that a dental hygienist is going to clean my teeth.

She cleans my teeth.

I rinse my mouth out with water when the hygienist is finished cleaning my teeth.

The dentist puts a sweet tasting liquid inside my mouth.
I leave the liquid in my mouth for a few minutes.
I rinse out my mouth.
My teeth feel smooth.
They look clean.
My visit to the dentist is over.

One time when I visited the dentist, he asked the dental assistant to take pictures of the inside of my teeth and gums.

When I had my pictures taken,

I sat in a special chair with a

large machine next to it.

I sat very still.

The assistant left the room.

I heard the machine go

"click."

The dentist looked at the pictures and found a cavity in one of my teeth.

He said that he needed to get rid of the cavity.

I went back to see the dentist so that he could get rid of the cavity on my tooth.

Once again I sat in the special chair and opened my mouth wide.

The dentist put something in my mouth so that it would not hurt when he worked in it.

The dentist put a plastic tube in my mouth so I wouldn't have to swallow.

He put some cotton by the tooth with the cavity.

The dentist used a tiny drill to get rid of the cavity.

There was a clean hole where the cavity used to be.

He filled up the hole with silver.

The dentist reminded me to take care of my teeth.
He told me to brush and floss my teeth every day.
Then he showed me how to do these things.

The dentist also reminded me

to eat good food and

not to eat too many sweets.

# helpful hints for parents about

# The Dentist

**Dear Parents:**

The purpose of this book is
- to give children the information they need about the dentist in order to dispel the fears that are created by "not knowing," and
- to give children control by encouraging and showing them how to become active participants in their visits to the dentist.

You can best implement the purpose of this book by
- reading it to your child, and
- reading the following *Helpful Hints* and using them whenever applicable.

# DENTISTRY

## Guide to dentists

The practice of dentistry can be divided into the following categories:
- **General dentistry.** This is the broadest division of dental practice. These dentists generally provide x-rays, cleaning, and basic restorative dental work. Patients are referred to other dentists for more specialized care.
- **Family dentistry.** These dentists cater to the dental care needs of both adults and children. Some families may prefer the convenience of all family members being cared for by the same dentist. Also, children cannot "grow out" of the family dentist's practice as they do with pedodontists.
- **Pedodontics.** These dentists specialize in children's dentistry. Pedodontists offer the advantages of experience, treating children's dental needs as well as a facility designed especially for children.

Other specialized dentists to whom your child over six might be referred:
- **Orthodontist**—straightens and aligns teeth.
- **Endontist**—performs root canal treatment.
- **Oral surgeon**—performs tooth extractions and surgery of the gums, mouth, and jaw.
- **Periodontist**—treats diseases of the gums.
- **Prosthodontist**—provides replacements for lost or damaged teeth.

## Choosing a dentist

To choose a dentist for your child, ask for a referral from one or more of the following:
- your child's doctor or health practitioner,
- the local organization of the American Dental Association, or
- a friend or relative who has a firsthand recommendation.

To make your selection of a dentist, do the following:
- Decide on several criteria that you will require in your child's dentist.

- Make a checklist of your criteria. These may include the following:
  1. dentist's experience
  2. length of practice
  3. availability in emergencies
  4. convenience of office location
  5. organization and staffing of the office
  6. fees
  7. attitude toward children
  8. rapport with your child
- Arrange a "visit" to the dentist for you and your child. Be sure to specify that you wish a brief interview with the dentist and a tour of his or her facilities.
- During the interview do the following:
  1. Ask both specific questions and open-ended questions which will provide the information necessary to make your choice.
  2. Encourage your child to ask questions.
  3. Observe your child's response to the dentist and vice versa.
- Evaluate the dentist on the basis of both your criteria *and* your feelings.

## A VISIT TO THE DENTIST

Request an appointment with the dentist of your choice for your child's dental examination.

### Before the visit

Plan for your child's dental visit by doing the following:
- Inform your child of the planned visit, and explain the procedures and experiences he or she might expect, such as
  1. having x-rays
  2. opening jaws wide
  3. cleaning with instruments
  4. rinsing
  5. flossing

- Answer your child's questions as completely as possible. Jot down your child's questions on a note pad to take with you to the dentist.
- Encourage your child to ask the dentist questions.
- Plan the appointment to fit into your child's routine of eating and napping. A tired or hungry child will not feel cooperative during an examination.

### In the waiting room

Many dentists, particularly child specialists, provide amusements for their young patients in the waiting room. To be prepared for a long wait or a crowded or boring waiting room, provide entertainment for your child. Some suggested amusements:
- doll or stuffed animal
- hand mirror
- drawing material
- necklaces (plastic pop beads)
- hand puppets
- small vehicles
- half-inflated balloon
- small books
- deck of cards (such as animal rummy)
- adhesive strip bandages
- colorful stickers and a blank book or card in which to stick them

These items can be carried and stored in a three-pound coffee can with a plastic lid, a purse with many compartments, or an interesting tote bag.

### The examination

Your child should actively participate in the dental examination and any other procedures which may follow.
- Have the dentist talk *to* your child as well as to you, the parent.
- Ask the dentist to inform the child about what to expect and which instruments will be used.

- Encourage your child to ask questions of the dentist, keeping in mind any questions he or she might have asked you previously.
- Do not leave your child alone with the dentist unless the child grants you his or her permission to leave.
- Be sure the dentist answers all of your child's questions honestly, accurately, and with sensitivity.
- Have the dentist make dental health recommendations directly to your child to be followed up at home between examinations.
- Make the visit to the dentist a positive experience by combining it with an enjoyable activity afterward.

## DENTAL HEALTH

Maintaining good dental health throughout your child's lifetime is a worthwhile goal of conscientious parents. Your child's teeth are a permanent feature which can contribute to or detract from your child's health, comfort, and appearance.

### Dental health problems

Common dental problems of young children:
- Cavities are the most common and preventable problem affecting 90 percent of children. If untreated, cavities can cause pain of toothache, infection, and early loss of baby or permanent teeth.
- Bumps and blows to baby and permanent teeth can cause serious damage or tooth loss. If your child's permanent tooth is knocked out whole, save it and seek emergency dental treatment immediately for the child and the tooth. If undamaged, the tooth may be replanted.
- Tooth loss that is premature or delayed for baby teeth can cause misalignment of permanent teeth.

### Cavity prevention

You can help prevent the formation of cavities in your child's teeth by doing the following:

- Form strong teeth in the bud stage through adequate prenatal nutrition for your child.
- Add fluoride supplements or fluoridated water to a healthy diet for your child. Fluoride strengthens tooth structure.
- Avoid putting your baby or young child to bed with a bottle. Formula, milk, and juices all contain sugar which collects on the teeth during sleep when the normal cleansing action of saliva is reduced.
- Discourage sticky or sugary foods which stay in contact with teeth longer than most food. These include dried fruits which are sticky and high in the natural sugar fructose.
- Clean your child's teeth regularly from the time the first one appears until your child gradually assumes responsibility for his or her own dental care.

## Dental care

Your child's dental care begins before birth with the mother's prenatal care and proper nutrition. Infants are born with two sets of teeth buds. The first tooth of the baby set usually begins to erupt before the child is six months old. The permanent teeth usually begin to appear in the sixth year. As each tooth appears, it must be cared for with good nutrition, regular cleaning, and professional care. Suggested dental care schedule:

*Birth to One Year*
- Clean baby's teeth and gums with gauze or a clean wash cloth.
- Use fluoride supplements to strengthen the tooth structure, making teeth more cavity resistant even before they erupt from the gums. Ask your child's health care professional about fluoride supplements or fluoridated water.

*One to Two Years*
- Brush your toddler's teeth daily.
- Introduce a small, soft toothbrush into your child's daily routine. Brushing at this age is imitative. Parents need to demonstrate good brushing habits.

*Two to Three Years*
- Brush and floss your child's teeth daily to establish the habit.
- Teach your child to brush and floss regularly.
- Begin regular professional dental care by taking your child to a dentist.

*Three to Six Years*
- Supervise and assist your child with daily brushing and flossing. Set a timer or play a favorite tape to assure adequate brushing time.
- Emphasize brushing after meals rather than only before bedtime.
- Encourage your child to choose healthful snacks between meals and to brush after eating or drinking sugary foods or beverages.
- Take your child to the dentist for checkups at least twice a year.